WORLD'S
SMALLEST
DINOSAURS

Rupert Matthews

Heinemann Library
Chicago, Illinois

www.capstonepub.com
Visit our website to find out
more information about
Heinemann-Raintree books.

To order:

☎ Phone 888-454-2279
💻 Visit www.capstonepub.com
    to browse our catalog and order online.

Edited by Rebecca Rissman and Laura Knowles
Designed by Richard Parker
Picture research by Mica Brancic
Originated by Capstone Global Library Ltd
Printed and bound in China by CTPS

15 14 13 12 11
10 9 8 7 6 5 4 3 2 1

Library of Congress Cataloging-in-Publication Data
Matthews, Rupert.
  World's smallest dinosaurs / Rupert Matthews.
    p. cm.—(Extreme dinosaurs)
  Includes bibliographical references and index.
  ISBN 978-1-4109-4526-6 (hb)—ISBN 978-1-4109-4533-4
(pb) 1. Dinosaurs—Juvenile literature. I. Title.
  QE861.5.M3747 2012
  567.9—dc23   2011016105

Acknowledgments
We would like to thank the following for permission to
reproduce images: © Capstone Publishers pp. **4** (James Field),
5 (James Field), **7** (James Field), **9** (James Field), **8** (Steve
Weston), **11** (Steve Weston), **10** (James Field), **13** (Steve
Weston), **12** (James Field), **14** (Steve Weston), **15** (Steve
Weston), **16** (James Field), **17** (James Field), **18** (James Field),
19 (James Field), **20** (James Field), **21** (Steve Weston), **23**
(Steve Weston), **22** (Steve Weston), **24** (James Field), **25** (Steve
Weston), **27** (James Field), **26** (James Field); Shutterstock p. **29**
(© Geoff Hardy).

Background design features reproduced with permission of
Shutterstock/© Szefei/© Fedorov Oleksiy/© Oleg Golovnev/
© Nuttakit.

Cover image of a *Sinosauropteryx* reproduced with permission
of © Capstone Publishers/James Field.

We would like to thank Nathan Smith for his invaluable help in
the preparation of this book.

Every effort has been made to contact copyright holders of
material reproduced in this book. Any omissions will be
rectified in subsequent printings if notice is given to the
publisher.

Disclaimer
All the Internet addresses (URLs) given in this book were valid
at the time of going to press. However, due to the dynamic
nature of the Internet, some addresses may have changed, or
sites may have changed or ceased to exist since publication.
While the author and publisher regret any inconvenience this
may cause readers, no responsibility for any such changes can
be accepted by either the author or the publisher.

Contents

Some words are shown in bold, **like this**.
You can find out what they mean by
looking in the glossary.

The Littlest Dinosaurs

Dinosaurs were a group of animals that lived millions of years ago. Some dinosaurs were the biggest animals ever to walk the Earth. But others were as small as a chicken! There were tiny dinosaurs of all kinds. There were small hunters, small plant eaters, and small **scavengers**. Some dinosaurs were so small that they ate insects.

5

Four-Winged Flyer

Microraptor was just under 2 feet long. That is about as long as a small dog. It probably hunted insects, worms, and other small animals.

Microraptor had short feathers on its body and long wing feathers. It looked a bit like a turkey! The feathers helped to keep it warm.

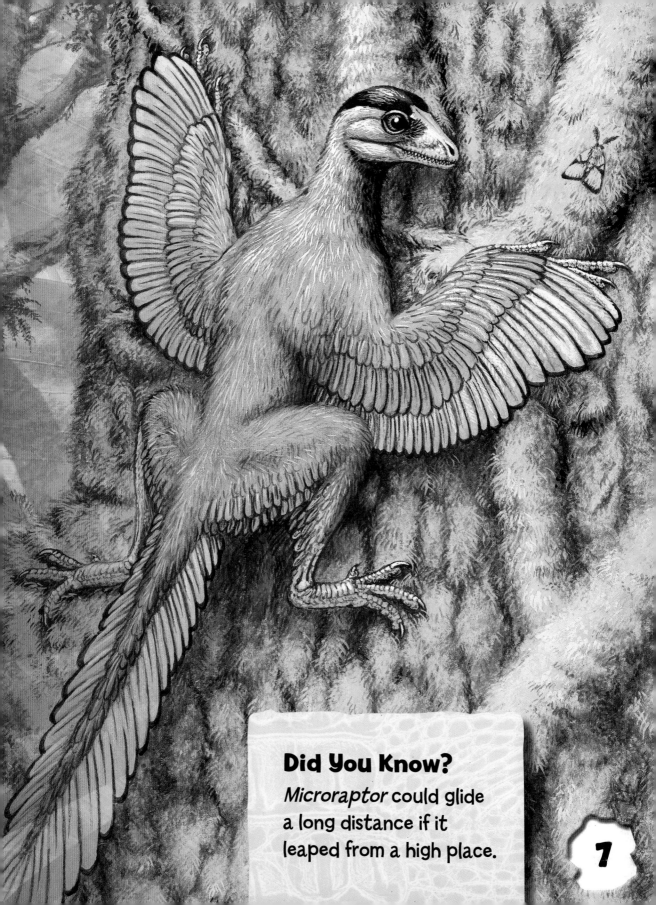

Did You Know?

Microraptor could glide a long distance if it leaped from a high place.

The Armored Pygmy

Ankylosaurian dinosaurs were heavy animals that were as big as tanks and covered in bone **armor**. But *Minmi* was less than 10 feet long—about the size of a horse. Large plates of bone with sharp points grew from its tail. If it was attacked by hunting dinosaurs, it would have swung its tail at them to drive them away.

"Compy"

The hunting **dinosaur** *Compsognathus* was about the size of a small turkey. It caught lizards, mammals, and bugs with its hands. Each hand was smaller than your thumb. It lived beside the sea where there were shallow **lagoons** and wide beaches. Its long legs and powerful muscles meant it could move quickly when hunting for food.

Did You Know?
Compsognathus is called "Compy" in the film **Jurassic** Park. No scientist ever uses this name.

Compsognathus

Tiny Hunters

The European **dinosaur** *Saltopus* was about the size of a small cat. It had hollow bones and weighed about 15 pounds. It walked on its back legs. The long, thin jaws contained dozens of small, sharp teeth. *Timimus* was a similar dinosaur that lived in Australia. The leg bones of *Timimus* are among the thinnest of all dinosaur bones.

Timimus

13

On the Plains

Lesothosaurus was a plant-eating **dinosaur** that lived on hot, dry plains in southern Africa. It was less than 3 feet long. That's about the same size as a dog. It had long legs so that it could run quickly to escape danger. When it stood upright it still would not have reached your knee.

Lesothosaurus

Did You Know?

Atlascopcosaurus was a similar dinosaur from Australia. The place where **fossils** of *Atlascopcosaurus* were found has been renamed "Dinosaur Cove."

Little Boneheads

The **dinosaur** with the longest name is *Micropachycephalosaurus,* but it was one of the smallest dinosaurs. It was less than 2 feet long. It had thick bone on top of its head. This may have been used to head-butt rivals in fights.

Scutellosaurus had bone plates along its back and on its head. Both of these dinosaurs were plant eaters that could walk on their back feet or on all fours.

Micropachycephalosaurus

Scutellosaurus

Colorful Hunter

The Asian **dinosaur** *Sinosauropteryx* was just over 3 feet long. Most of that length was the long, thin tail. It was covered in small feathers that would have helped keep it warm. **Fossils** of the dinosaur's feathers show that *Sinosauropteryx* had dark stripes on its body and tail. The back of the animal was probably yellowish or reddish in color.

Bambiraptor

The hunting **dinosaur** *Bambiraptor* stood about a foot tall. Even if it stretched, it would not have been able to reach much higher than your knee! Its front legs ended in three strong claws that it used to grab **prey**. *Bambiraptor* belonged to a group of raptors who had bigger brains than some other dinosaurs, so it was possibly smarter than other dinosaurs.

Did You Know?
Bambiraptor was named after Bambi. This was a baby deer that appeared in a film made in 1942.

Shield Faces

Ceratopsian dinosaurs are famous for having long horns on their heads and bone shields over their necks. Strong muscles connected to the shield worked the jaws. However, the smallest ceratopsians had no horns at all. *Graciliceratops* was just over 3 feet long. *Protoceratops* was the size of a pony. It walked on all four legs and had a neck shield.

Protoceratops

Did You Know?
Graciliceratops walked on its hind legs.

neck shield

Graciliceratops

23

Special Teeth

Some small **dinosaurs** had special teeth for eating certain foods. *Incisivosaurus* was a little over 3 feet long, about the length of a labrador dog. It had long teeth in the front of its mouth. It may have used these teeth to reach seeds in pine cones or to get at other seeds or nuts. *Archaeoceratops* had a narrow beak. This may have been used to bite leaves off palms or ferns.

Incisivosaurus

Archaeoceratops

Leaping for Insects

Protarchaeopteryx could grow to be over 6 feet long. Its body was about the size of a large goose. It had long feathers on its arms and on its tail. Some scientists think that it could leap into the air to catch flying insects. The feathers may have helped it stay in the air. Others think it ran around catching food on the ground. The feathers might have been used to display to other **dinosaurs**.

How to Become a Museum Curator

A museum curator is the person who is in charge of museum collections. The curator decides what objects should be on display and when the museum will be open. Most curators have been to college. They will also have done **research** work about a particular subject. They might have looked into the **Mesozoic Era**, also known as the "Age of **Dinosaurs**." They will probably have worked at the museum, showing people around and explaining the display to visitors.

Glossary

ankylosaurians family of armored, plant-eating dinosaurs that lived between 160 and 65 million years ago

armor outer shell or bone on some dinosaurs that protected their bodies

ceratopsian family of horned, plant-eating dinosaurs that lived in North America and Asia toward the end of the Age of Dinosaurs

dinosaur group of animals that lived on land millions of years ago during the Mesozoic Era

fossil part of a plant or animal that has been buried in rocks for millions of years

Jurassic part of Earth's history that began about 200 million years ago and ended about 145 million years ago

lagoon shallow body of salt water near the sea, surrounded by sandbanks

Mesozoic Era part of Earth's history that is sometimes called the "Age of Dinosaurs." It is divided into three periods: Triassic, Jurassic, and Cretaceous.

prey animal that is killed by another for food

research study of a particular subject such as dinosaurs

scavengers animals that feed on dead animals

Find Out More

Books

Bingham, Caroline. *Dinosaur Encyclopedia.* New York: Dorling
    Kindersley, 2009.
Lessem, Don. *The Ultimate Dinopedia.* Washington, DC: National
    Geographic Children's Books, 2010.
Markarian, Margie. *Who Cleans Dinosaur Bones?* Chicago:
    Heinemann-Raintree, 2010.
Matthews, Rupert. *Ripley Twists: Dinosaurs.* Orlando, FL: Ripley
    Publishing, 2010.

Websites

science.nationalgeographic.com/science/prehistoric-world.html
Learn more about dinosaurs and other facts about the prehistoric
world at this National Geographic Website.

www.ucmp.berkeley.edu/
Learn more about fossils, prehistoric times, and paleontology
at this Website of the University of California Museum of
Paleontology.

www.nhm.ac.uk/kids-only/dinosaurs
The Natural History Museum is located in London, England. Its
Website has a lot of information about dinosaurs, including facts,
quizzes, and games.

www.kidsdinos.com/
Play dinosaur games and read about dinosaurs on this Website.

Index